Also available in this series from Quadrille:

MINDFULNESS
MINDFULNESS II
QUIET
FRIENDSHIP
LOVE
CONFIDENCE
TIDINESS
HAPPINESS
LUCK
US

To Anna

the little book of
MOTHERHOOD

you are going to
be an amazing
mummy. All my love
Unce Keith Aunty Cath

Hardie Grant

QUADRILLE

xxx

"Womanliness means only motherhood; All love begins and ends there..."

ROBERT BROWNING

From *The Inn Album, Park VII*

4

Motherhood: because privacy is over-rated.

"No language can express the power, and beauty, and heroism and majesty of a mother's love."

E. H. CHAPIN
From *Living Words*

Motherhood is infinitely hard to describe in words, for its currency is love. It's a feeling that surpasses all others; a need to care, a need to guide and nurture. Most of all it's holding your child's heart in your hands, always.

*"Of all the rights of women,
the greatest is to be a mother."*

LIN YUTANG

Dictionary definition of 'motherhood'

1. The state of being a mother.

2. The qualities or spirit of a mother.

3. Mothers collectively.

"Mother is a verb. It's something you do, not just who you are."

DOROTHY CANFIELD

The origin of 'motherhood'

The word was first recorded between 1375–1425, and comes from the Middle English word *moderhed*.

"Because I feel that, in the
      Heavens above,
The angels, whispering to one
      another,
Can find, among their
      burning terms of love,
None so devotional as that of
      'Mother'."

EDGAR ALLEN POE
From *To My Mother*

Motherhood – the facts

- There are two billion mothers in the world – that's a lot of love, tears and nappies.

- Every second, 4.3 babies are born.

- A woman's chance of having twins is one in 32. Her chance of having triplets or higher multiples is one in 540.

- An average baby has around 4,700 nappy changes by the age of two.

" The babe at first feeds upon the mother's bosom, but it is always on her heart."

HENRY WARD BEECHER

UNICEF's top-five countries in which to give birth

1. Japan
2. Iceland
3. Singapore
4. Finland
5. Slovenia and Estonia

In 1967, 49 per cent of mothers were stay-at-home mothers, a figure that steadily dropped through the decades until 1999, when only 23 per cent of mothers stayed at home. Since then, the percentage of mothers who stay at home has risen slightly and was recorded at 29 per cent in 2012.

Stay-at-home mothers spend an average of 16.5 hours a week doing household chores. Working mothers tend to spend around eight hours a week on the same tasks.

Scandinavian mothers are considered among the happiest in the world, with a year's paid maternity leave and a relaxed, hands-off attitude to parenting that allows children to be more independent.

Danish motherhood is about encouraging children to explore and get close to nature while forging their own identity.

Denmark, which is almost consistently ranked in the top-three happiest countries in the world, is recognised as one of the best places to raise children.

"*My mother had a good deal of trouble with me, but I think she enjoyed it.*"

MARK TWAIN

From *The Autobiography of Mark Twain*

There is no 'right' age to become a mother. Biologically, the best age is late teens to early twenties, as this is when a woman is in optimum health. Sociologically, the best age is somewhat older. In truth, the right and best age for motherhood is when a woman is ready.

Motherhood is a literal brain changer. Scientists have discovered that new mums have significantly more grey matter post-birth. This is thought to be because of the influx of hormones during pregnancy.

Mother and child share more than an emotional bond; they share cells too. The cell swap happens during pregnancy through the placenta, but evidence suggests that cells can stay in the mother's body for years afterwards, meaning she literally carries a part of her child with her.

"If you desire to drain to the dregs the fullest cup of scorn and hatred that a fellow human creature can pour out for you, let a young mother hear you call dear baby 'it'."

JEROME K. JEROME

Talking to your unborn baby helps its brain to grow. The mother's heartbeat and the sound of her voice are enough to trigger significant development.

Motherhood is like falling in love. While oxytocin, the 'cuddle hormone' responsible for those maternal feelings, floods the body during pregnancy, it also occurs post-birth whenever a mother looks at her child or hears it cry. This same hormone occurs when we fall in love, which explains the overwhelming emotions mums feel on meeting their newborns.

"*A mother's love is something
that no one can explain –
It is made of deep devotion
and of sacrifice and pain.
It is endless and unselfish
and enduring, come what may,
For nothing can destroy it
or take that love away.*"

HELEN STEINER RICE
From *A Mother's Love*

Babies acquire their mother's experiences, learning fear at a young age from the odour their mums produce when they are in fight-or-flight mode.

"*Mother's love is bliss, is peace. It need not be acquired, it need not be deserved.*"

ERICH FROMM

From *The Art of Loving*

What is a mother?

She is not one thing, but everything.

She is the sun, moon and stars, the very universe of her newborn. A well of unconditional love, freely giving, nurturing and inspiring.

She is the welcome smile, the guiding light and the rock from which comfort and balance can be found.

She is different things to different people, but she is yours to be treasured, respected and cherished.

Mothers are not made, they just are: emerging when a child is born to provide warmth, shelter and strength unreservedly.

"*A mother is the truest friend we have, when trials, heavy and sudden, fall upon us; when adversity takes the place of prosperity; when friends who rejoice with us in our sunshine desert us; when trouble thickens around us, still will she cling to us, and endeavour with her kind precepts and counsels to dissipate the darkness, and cause peace to return to our hearts.*"

WASHINGTON IRVING

What's in a name?

In English she's called mum, mom or mummy, the Spanish say mama, as do the Chinese. In Iceland, it's mamma, while it's ma in Punjabi, and me in Vietnamese. This is no coincidence. Babies around the world tend to find 'ma' easier to vocalise in those early stages, which is why most countries have taken this as their lead to create a word for 'mother'.

"*She openeth her mouth with wisdom; and in her tongue is the law of kindness. She looketh well to the ways of her household. And eateth not the bread of idleness. Her children arise up, and call her blessed; her husband also, and he praiseth her.*"

THE KING JAMES BIBLE
Proverbs 31:26-28

Mum, mom and mam – all shortened versions of mother. It doesn't matter which you choose, so long as it's said with love.

No instruction book

You said 'ma-ma' at ten months old,
melting my anxious heart.
I'd coped with nappies, sleepless
nights –would the rewards now start?

When you were two how pleased I was
with 'Mummy' as my name.
Toddler tantrums, fights with food,
I loved you just the same.

You turned into a teenager.
"Enough said," some folks say.
And yet despite the darkest days
you grew and found your way.

Now you're grown up and I am 'Mum';
how did that come to be?
Who knows? But I am sure of this:
the name sounds good to me.

VIV APPLE

"I think my life began with waking up and loving my mother's face..."

GEORGE ELIOT
From *Daniel Deronda*

"Children are the anchors that hold a mother to life."

SOPHOCLES
From *Phaedra*

MOM on its head,
is WOW, enough said.

"Motherhood was the great equaliser for me; I started to identify with everybody... as a mother, you have that impulse to wish that no child should ever be hurt, or abused, or go hungry, or not have opportunities in life."

ANNIE LENNOX

Motherhood is not a rite of passage, it's an approach, an attitude, a way of being. Giving birth is not essential to being 'in the hood'.

Motherhood does not judge, it is beyond age, race, religion and politics. Simply put, it is what it is, whoever you are. There is no one ideal, every mother makes a sacrifice. Every mother counts.

"Biology is the least of what makes someone a mother."

OPRAH WINFREY

Make a list of the all the wonderful women you know, including yourself and next to each name write down at least three qualities that make them top mamma material. Whether they're mothers or not, it doesn't matter, it's about recognising the nurturing power of motherhood in all of us.

There is no epidural for motherhood.

"A mother's arms are made of tenderness and children sleep soundly in them."

VICTOR HUGO

Motherhood and the five 'e's

Motherhood is emotional

It's a rollercoaster ride from start to finish, where the highs are so high you might literally fly, and the lows can sweep you down to the depths of the earth.

Motherhood is exhausting

Some days will pass without you knowing. Some days you'll wonder how you keep going. Sleep is the Holy Grail. Stealing a nap becomes a secret treasure.

Motherhood is endless

This is the one ride you cannot get off, even though at times you might want to. Ultimately you are connected forever in the eternal dance of love.

Motherhood is exciting

Each moment an adventure, an opportunity to learn and marvel and watch this little life you've carefully crafted take flight.

Motherhood is exceptional

There is nothing else like it, and never will be. It stands alone: a selfless act of heroism.

A mother's love is unconditional...
her temper is another story.

"What a mother sings to the cradle goes all the way down to the coffin."

HENRY WARD BEECHER

Tips for new mothers

- The demands of motherhood on body and brain are never-ending so make the most of peaceful moments while your baby's asleep. The average newborn sleeps around 16 hours a day, sometimes more. Use this time to relax and rest.

- Catnaps work for mothers as well as felines, so perfect the art of dozing off when you have five minutes.

- Listen to advice with an open mind, but do what feels right. You're a mother and mothers always know best.

- Ask for help and take up offers of support. Don't try to be Wonder Woman!

- Being a mother takes energy, so above all else make time to eat something delicious and nutritious.

- Don't judge yourself. Motherhood is not a competition or a race. You don't have to win or be the best – just be you.

- Celebrate the small victories: having a shower, getting dressed, making a drink or catching forty winks.

- Don't let worry take over. It's understandable to feel anxious, but you've got this!

> *"New mothers enter the world of parenting feeling much like Alice in Wonderland."*

DEBRA GILBERT ROSENBERG

Becoming a mother

'M' no longer stands for **me**,
it stands for **mother**.

Motherhood and selflessness

It's impossible to be a selfish mother. Like oil and water, the two don't mix.

"The natural state of motherhood is unselfishness. When you become a mother, you are no longer the centre of your own universe. You relinquish that position to your children."

JESSICA LANGE

"I supposed a mother is one to whom you hurry when you are troubled."

EMILY DICKINSON

Motherhood is like a tree, with roots anchored deep in the earth. As a mum, you provide balance and strength, a safe haven and a place where your child can rest under the shade of your loving touch. Then, when they're ready to fly, you stretch out those branches, give them a helping hand and encourage them to follow their dreams. Inspire them to dance with the clouds and watch the patterns they create in the sky, but should they falter or fall or simply need a moment, they can return to the safety of your boughs. You are there in all weathers, standing tall. Timeless. Majestic. Mother.

*"All that I am, or hope to be,
I owe to my angel mother."*

ABRAHAM LINCOLN

Mothers are guardian angels.

Move over Marvel: there's a new superhero in town. She's mighty, fierce, irrepressible – a mover of worlds. She is the mother. Always strong. Always there. Always right.

"*My mother said to me, "If you are a soldier, you will become a general. If you are a monk, you will become the Pope." Instead, I was a painter, and became Picasso.*"

PABLO PICASSO

"Motherhood is the ultimate call to sacrifice."

WANGECHI MUTU

Shower, hair and make-up in under 10 minutes (and with an audience): that's motherhood.

Motherhood is ...

- Always having snacks
- 24/7
- Never forgetting babywipes
- Rewarding
- Knowing how to change nappies anywhere
- Tiring
- Becoming very used to mess
- Not a soft skill
- Heavenly (especially when they're all asleep)

Motherhood makes you kinder. You become more aware of those around you because you stop thinking about and putting yourself first. This causes a shift in perspective and you're able to see the bigger picture.

Be kind to yourself. Look after body, mind and soul by eating nourishing food. Take time out to relax and de-stress and allow some space to explore and experience the things you love.

Motherhood rebuilds you. Piece by piece it transforms you into who you need to be. As with any renovation, there will be mess – lots of it!

Motherhood can feel lonely. It's the liquid darkness of early-morning feeds when all the world's asleep, or so it seems. Then there's only you responsible for the tiny beating heart cradled in your arms. This is when the greatest realisation occurs, and you know that nothing else matters. The sky could fall in, the world could split in two, but in this moment you have everything you need.

Expect the unexpected. Every day brings a new surprise, a puzzle, sometimes a miracle. Motherhood is heart-stopping.

"*The heart of a mother is a deep abyss at the bottom of which you will always find forgiveness.*"

HONORÉ DE BALZAC

"I want my children to have all the things I couldn't afford. Then I want to move in with them."

PHYLLIS DILLER

Essential motherhood skill number one: a sense of humour. It helps mums navigate the insanity that becomes daily routine. The ability to laugh at yourself when the going gets tough swiftly follows.

Find something to laugh about every day. To help you see the funny side of motherhood, replay what happened in your mind but imagine it's a comedy sketch. When we observe events from the outside, we see the humour and can detach from the stress of the situation.

You realise very soon into motherhood that sticky fingers and messy mouths are always around the corner.

You know you're in the midst of motherhood when nipping to the local shop by yourself feels like a vacation.

*"My mother loved children.
She would have given anything
if I had been one."*

GROUCHO MARX

Motherhood is like going back to school, but the roles are reversed. You are the teacher at the front of the class. It's your job to guide, support and impart the wisdom, and while this might seem scary, it's about going back to basics, trusting your instincts and letting your heart take the lead.

"Mama was my greatest teacher, a teacher of compassion, love and fearlessness. If love is sweet as a flower, then my mother is that sweet flower of love."

STEVIE WONDER

"*The mother's heart is the child's schoolroom.*"

HENRY WARD BEECHER

Motherhood makes you clever. While you might feel in a total spin, and generally exhausted, research shows that pregnancy and child-rearing boosts intelligence by building up the brain. A large number of neurons and neuronal connections double, which improves brain function and the ability to think coherently. Studies show that both motivation and memory excel, while emotional intelligence and mental acuity also progress.

"*When your mother asks, "Do you want a piece of advice?" it is a mere formality. It doesn't matter if you answer yes or no. You're going to get it anyway.*"

ERMA BOMBECK

"A mother is she who can take the place of all others, but whose place no one else can take."

CARDINAL GASPARD MERMILLOD

The mother's connection to her child starts as a physical one, but once the umbilical cord is cut, a different bond forms, one that trumps all other ties because it is infinite and timeless. From those first tentative steps we take as a babe until we blossom into adulthood, this connection is crucial. It helps form our sense of self, and just like the earth sustains its wildlife, it gives us a solid base from which we can grow. This goes some way to explain the difficulty some of us encounter when attempting to break those ties and find our own way in the world.

In many cultures there are specific rituals to help youngsters cut the apron strings and make the transition into adulthood. In some traditions, children, especially boys who were considered the warriors of the group, were removed from their mother at a tender age and made to live with other young men – a harsh experience for all, but the ancients recognised the power and influence of the mother archetype, and in some cases feared the effect it might have on their fledgling sons.

"She never quite leaves her children at home, even when she doesn't take them along."

MARGARET CULKIN BANNING

" When we recognise the virtues, the talent, the beauty of Mother Earth, something is born in us, some kind of connection; love is born."

THICH NHAT HANH

Mother nature – the ultimate mummy

From lush green landscapes and tumbling hills to golden vistas and swelling seas, she made it all. The ancient Greeks called her Gaia, the Native Americans, Mother Earth. She is known by many other names, the common thread being that from her eternal womb all life sprang forth. Associated with healing and harmony, this primordial being exists to protect the earth and everything upon it. When we look after our environment, we honour Mother Nature and all that she does for us.

"Sometimes the strength of motherhood is greater than natural laws."

BARBARA KINGSOLVER

Put the 'm' in motherhood

Like any wise mamma, Mother Nature can guide us during our personal journey into motherhood. Whatever your situation, connecting with her helps develop your nurturing instincts, giving you the M(otherhood) Factor!

Get gardening

Whether you pot a few plants, grow some herbs, or volunteer at your local allotment, cultivating the land in whatever form you choose brings you closer to Mother Nature, and to the mother archetype within.

"*As it turns out one of the most wonderful joys of motherhood is the other mothers.*"

ANNA JORDAN

You are not alone – motherhood is a collective, a club, a sisterhood. Make time for other mothers. Learn from them. Appreciate them. Most importantly, have fun with them.

If you don't already, pencil in regular 'mummy' play dates. Make these occasions where you get together solely as women and mothers, and do something you enjoy, like dancing, going for a run, learning a new skill or just hanging out with tea and cake. There doesn't have to be an agenda; this is about much-deserved togetherness.

"*God could not be everywhere,
and therefore he made mothers.*"

JEWISH PROVERB

Mothers and deities

In ancient times mothers turned to the gods for assistance when it came to childbirth, petitioning them for a safe delivery and their child's protection. In ancient Egypt women would squat on a brick to give birth; this was often adorned with symbols and images of the cow-headed goddess Hathor, who was associated with motherhood. The Greeks turned to Eileithyia the Greek goddess of childbirth and labour pains, while Norse women put their trust in the deity Frigg to watch over them during childbirth.

Mother deities exist throughout folklore. These powerful goddesses encompass the varying aspects of motherhood, and together illustrate the power of a mother's love.

Juno, the mediator mother

The Roman goddess Juno is a mediator mother. Associated with marriage, conception and pregnancy, she also governed finances and was petitioned by Roman warriors for her assistance in battle. Like any good mother, she juggled many different roles and was an expert in negotiation; because of this she was often called upon to settle marital disputes and disagreements. Community was everything to Juno, and this was reflected in the number of temples and shrines built in her honour.

Isis, the trickster mother

The Egyptian goddess Isis, also referred to as the 'Mother of Life', was a mistress of magic. She used her infinite wisdom to obtain the powers of the sun god Ra, and created a snake out of mud and saliva, which delivered a fatal bite to the god. She then offered to heal him, but to do so she needed his secret name and the key to his magical abilities. A desperate Ra revealed his name to her and she healed him, thus becoming the most powerful goddess in Egypt. Being a mother goddess, she used this power to care and protect her people.

Kali, the warrior mother

The Hindu goddess Kali is a scary figure. She may be associated with death and destruction, but really her concerns are with the death of the ego. Extremely protective, this mother goddess considers all humans to be her children. Pictured wearing a garland of skulls and a skirt of dismembered arms, her terrifying appearance is believed to repel evil and provide liberation for her followers. Thought to be the womb where all things were born and ultimately return in death, she represents the cycle of life.

Kwan Yin, the caring mother

The Chinese mother goddess Kwan Yin is synonymous with creation. Able to hear the cries of the world, and particularly those of children in anguish, she took this suffering upon herself to ease their pain. She is often pictured holding the pearls of illumination in one hand as a symbol of her judgement and compassion, and a vase containing 'sweet dew' in the other. She poured this concoction, thought to be the nectar of wisdom, upon the earth so that her children could experience true peace.

"Mother is the name for God in the lips and hearts of little children."

WILLIAM MAKEPEACE THACKERAY
From *Vanity Fair*

Harness your inner mother goddess

Whatever stage you're at in life or as a mother, you can call on your inner mother goddess for strength, energy and clarity. So if you're feeling stressed or anxious, take a moment to unleash the feminine force within.

- Place the palms of both hands over the centre of your chest.

- Breathe deeply and close your eyes.

- Imagine a pink gemstone in the centre of your chest. See it sparkling and radiating light.

- As you breathe in, imagine the stone getting bigger. As you breathe out, imagine it getting brighter.

- Spend a few minutes focusing on each breath and picturing the glow of the jewel in your heart.

- Know that you can face anything, do anything and be anything!

"...for there is a religion in all deep love, but the love of a Mother is, at your age, the veil of a softer light between the Heart and the Heavenly Father!"

SAMUEL TAYLOR COLERIDGE
From *Letter XXII to 'My Dear Friend'*

Mothers are magical; they turn tears into laughter, pain into hope and a smile into a new beginning.

"When Mother smiled, no matter how nice her face had been before, it became incomparably nicer and everything around seemed to brighten up as well."

LEO TOLSTOY

From *Childhood, Boyhood, Youth*

Tell your mother you love her...

Te amo, Mamá.

Je t'aime, Maman.

Ich liebe dich, Mama.

Voglio bene alla tua, Mamma.

Kocham cię, Mamo.

Wǒ ài nǐ, Māmā.

Eu te amo, Mãe.

Con yêu, Mẹ.

Ik hou van je, Mam.

Motherhood mantras

Get your motherhood mojo on by repeating these mantras daily.

- This is my motherhood: I do it my way!

- The moment maketh the mother. I enjoy each moment for what it is.

- Kindness is the currency of motherhood.

- Breathe, smile, repeat.

- I am enough.

- Motherhood is a journey, not a destination.

- The power of motherhood is mine!

- I am Mother: hear me roar!

Q: The golden secret of motherhood?

A: Ask your mum.

*" It was the rainbow gave thee birth,
and left thee all her lovely hues."*

W. H. DAVIES

Birthing: traditions and customs

Women have been giving birth since the beginning of time, but the traditions and customs that are associated with childbirth vary around the world, making those first steps into motherhood a unique and magical experience.

Brazil

Generous new mothers give gifts to those who come to see them and their new baby in hospital. Most other parts of the world do it the other way round, with visitors bringing presents for the infant, but in Brazil, the mother shares her love and appreciation with a token of thanks.

Turkey

Shortly after giving birth, new mothers are served with a drink called *lohusa serbeti*. This vibrant concoction combines cinnamon, sugar and red food colouring to give it a distinct hue. A celebratory tipple, it's also served to visitors so they can toast the new arrival.

Nigeria

A sense of community is vital to Nigerian women, so it's common practice for the baby's grandmother to give the child its first bath. This ritual, known as *omugwo*, is a gesture of love that demonstrates that the new mother is not on her own, but is supported by a close network of women.

Japan

The Japanese mother sees childbirth as a natural, peaceful time, which continues after the baby is born. For three weeks the mother will remain in a cocoon of love with her baby, looked after by her parents and other family members. Usually with complete bed rest, she will be pampered and allowed to bond with her infant in solitude.

Latin America

Just as in Japan, Latin American mothers are also given the chance to bond with their babies in seclusion. This peaceful period of time, known as *la cuarentena*, usually lasts for six weeks. The new mother abstains from all sexual activity, limits certain foods and focuses solely on breastfeeding her baby, while family and friends share out the chores.

Bali

Once the mother has given birth, her placenta is swiftly spirited away and cleaned. It is then placed in a box and buried deep in the earth. The placenta is considered alive, and in some cases the twin of the new infant, although some suggest it represents the baby's guardian angel. Either way, it's treated with the utmost respect.

New Zealand

Also fans of burying the placenta, the Maoris practise this in the hope that it provides the child with a spiritual connection to the land.

Gambia and Senegal

It's common practice to see new mothers turn their heads away from their newborns in an attempt to trick the gods. They make it look like their new arrivals are unimportant, in the hope that their souls aren't taken. This protective reflex has its roots in superstition, but is also due partly to the high mortality rate of infants, caused by poor living conditions and a lack of medical equipment.

"A woman has two smiles that an angel might envy: the smile that accepts a lover before words are uttered, and the smile that lights on the firstborn baby, and assures it of a mother's love."

THOMAS C. HALIBURTON

" *Whatever else is unsure in this stinking dunghill of a world, a mother's love is not.* "

JAMES JOYCE
From *A Portrait of the Artist as a Young Man*

Mother's Day

Mothering Sunday was first celebrated in the UK in the 16th century. At the time this was a religious festival in line with the Christian calendar and had nothing to do with real mothers. Instead, those celebrating would visit their 'mother' church and eat simnel cake. Thanks to Constance Smith, it experienced a revival from 1913 onwards. She was inspired by Anna Jarvis, an American who founded Mother's Day in the United States on 10 May 1908, as a way of honouring her own mother; the day was officially recognised by Congress in 1914.

Constance produced a booklet titled *The Revival of Mothering Sunday* in 1920. This marked a turning point, and is the basis of the celebration today.

"With what price we pay for the glory of motherhood."

ISADORA DUNCAN

To the world you are a mother, but to your family you are the world.

Mother's Day around the world

In Mexico, Mother's Day, also known as *Dia de las Madres*, falls on the 10 May, whatever day of the week this happens to be. This is a grand occasion, which begins with mothers being serenaded by *mariachi* bands. There are banquets, dancing and lots of music. Flowers also play a big part in the celebrations.

In the the Balkans, Mother's Day is an excuse to have some fun. Held over a three-day period in December, which includes Children's Day and Father's Day, it's customary for children to sneak into their mother's bedroom and tie her up. To be released, she must offer them gifts. This role is reversed on Children's Day, when the children are tied up and must promise to behave!

Jasmine is the flower of choice in Thailand, and the most popular gift on Mother's Day, which falls on 12 August to mark the birthday of Queen Sirikit.

In France the *Fête des Mères* falls on the fourth Sunday in May but can be put back a week when this overlaps with Pentecost. Flowers, chocolates and cards are a big part of the celebrations.

The Japanese originally celebrated their mothers on the birthday of the Empress Koujun, known as *Haha no hi*, but this has since been changed to the second Sunday in May. During this time Japanese mothers are showered with gifts, including red carnations, scarves and handkerchiefs. It's also common for younger children to sketch illustrations and name them 'My Mother'. These are then submitted for an exhibition.

Swedish Mother's Day falls on the last Sunday in May. Children sell plastic flowers, and the money raised is used to send mothers with small children on a short break away.

In Ethiopia, Mother's Day is celebrated at the end of the rainy season, when the first rays of sunshine appear. A celebratory meal is prepared, with daughters contributing vegetables, cheese and spices, while sons bring different types of meat to the feast.

Although Mother's Day falls on the last Sunday in November, most Russians prefer to honour this festival on 8 March, as part of International Women's Day.

Top treats for mothers

Whether you're a mother, about to become one, or want to celebrate the matriarchs in your life, these tips and treats make motherhood the only team worth joining!

- Make a motherhood memory box. Find a special container and fill it with mementos, from scans and pictures, to locks of hair, drawings from child to mother, cherished treasures from time spent together, and anything that says 'motherhood' to you on a personal level. Whether you're the mother, or you're making it for your own, fill it with love and keep adding to it.

- Write a letter to your mother. Put pen to paper, rather than going digital, and open your heart. Tell your mother something you've never told her before. Tell her why she's so amazing, then give it to her whenever you like. You don't need to wait for a special occasion to let her know how much she means to you.

- If you're just embarking on the journey of motherhood, write a letter to your child. You might not have met them yet but let them know how much they mean to you, your hopes for them and how cherished they are. Seal it with kiss and keep it as a gift, for when they're older.

- Bake a 'Mother's Cake'. This could be your mother's recipe, something you've created to mark your passage into motherhood and that you'll pass on to your children, or just a cake to share with the mothers in your social group. Enjoy with your nearest and dearest.

- Go for a walk with your mother. This could be somewhere you both like and have memories of, or somewhere new that you can explore together. Use this time to share your thoughts, have fun and reconnect.

"When I stopped seeing my mother through the eyes of a child, I saw the woman who helped me give birth to myself."

NANCY FRIDAY

From *My Mother, Myself*

Life doesn't come with a manual,
it comes with a mother.

"Mothers are all slightly insane."

J.D. SALINGER
From *The Catcher in the Rye*

Motherhood – sayings and proverbs

There is only one pretty child in the world, and every mother has it.

CHINESE PROVERB

A rich child often sits in a poor mother's lap.

DANISH PROVERB

In every woman there is a queen. Speak to the queen and the queen will answer.

NORWEGIAN PROVERB

God could not be everywhere
and therefore he made mothers.

JEWISH PROVERB

What the daughter does,
the mother did.

JEWISH PROVERB

Who takes the child by the hand takes
the mother by the heart.

GERMAN PROVERB

Heaven is under the feet of mothers.

PERSIAN PROVERB

The greater love is a mother's; then come dog's; then a sweetheart's.

POLISH PROVERB

An ounce of mother is worth a pound of clergy.

SPANISH PROVERB

*"We are born of love;
love is our mother."*

RUMI

The beautiful quest

Being a mother is a vocation, not a job. It's a calling and there is no end to the quest. The Holy Grail is already in your hands; it's up to you to keep it safe and treasure it above all others. The road will be long, and fraught with obstacles. There will be times you feel like giving up, but equally there will be times when you're overcome with joy, when just a single word and smile can make your heart burst with love. Motherhood is a wholly spiritual experience, a sacred passage that touches your soul, fills you with divine light and changes you forever.

"I can imagine no heroism greater than motherhood."

LANCE CONRAD
From *The Price of Creation*

The days may feel long, but the years go by in a heartbeat.

Where once you were the picture, in motherhood, you become the frame.

In a tradition parallel to the American establishment of Mother's Day, servant girls in large English country houses were given the day off to visit their mothers. Picking wild flowers on their way home, led to the tradition of posies still being offered to mothers at churches on Mothering Sunday today.

Folk cultures assign meaning to flowers. These blooms relate to motherhood.

Pink carnations: symbolise a mother's love.

Jasmine: suggest unconditional and eternal love.

Azaleas: are the Chinese flower for womanhood.

Pink roses: represent a caring nature.

Wisdom of the stones suggests that certain jewels represent aspects of motherhood.

Rose quartz: represents eternal love.

Garnet: symbolises love between family members.

Tanzanite: symbolic of the gift of life.

Zircon: believed to have the power to relieve pain.

A woman is not a mother by the number of children she has, but by the amount of love she stores in her heart.

Matronalia was a festival dedicated to the fertility of married women in Ancient Rome. Celebrated on the first day of March, married women participated in rituals at the temple of Juno Lucina (the goddess of childbirth). At home, wives received gifts from their husbands, and women prepared a meal for the female servants, who were given a day off.

Marvellous
Out of this world
Terrifying
Humbling
Exciting
Radiant
Heart-stopping
Overwhelming
Outstanding
Dazzling

Proust's seven volume, *Remembrance of Things Past* describes in exquisite detail the longing of a small boy for his mother to kiss him goodnight. If you can't face reading all one million words, seek out the early section in volume one, for an almost perfect description of the pull of a mother over a child:

"*My sole consolation when I went upstairs for the night was that Mamma would come in and kiss me after I was in bed. But this good night lasted for so short a time, she went down again so soon, that the moment in which I heard her climb the stairs, and then caught the sound of her garden dress of blue muslin, from which hung little tassels of plaited straw, rustling along the double-doored corridor, was for me a moment of the utmost pain; for it heralded the moment which was to follow it, when she would have left me and gone downstairs again.*"

MARCEL PROUST

"*It's not what you do for your children but what you have taught them to do for themselves that will make them successful human beings.*"

ANN LANDER

"Children learn more from what you are than what you teach."

W.E.B. DU BOIS

To be a mother is to expand your sense of self; to expand to the very limits of your life.

"Children are not a distraction from more important work. They are the most important work."

C.S. LEWIS

Some of the earliest works of pre-historic art feature the wide-hipped, heavy-bosomed figures of the 'mother goddess'. Even those cave-dwelling hunter-gatherer tribes knew the power contained within the mother archetype.

Seven sacred mothers:

Demeter, Ancient Greek earth mother.
Durga, the Hindu supreme mother goddess.
Isis, Egyptian goddess of motherhood, single mother to Horus.
Mary, mother of Jesus.
Mother Tara, the Buddhist mother goddess.
Pachamama, the Andean mother earth goddess.
Sarah, the Jewish matriarch who gave birth to Isaac.

Seven fictional mothers:

Ma, *Little House on the Prairie.*
Marge Simpson, *The Simpsons.*
Margaret 'Marmee' , *Little Women.*
Maria, *The Sound of Music.*
Marilla, *Anne of Green Gables.*
Molly Weasley, *Harry Potter.*
Morticia Adams, *The Addams Family.*

Mothers who rule:

Benazir Bhutto, was the first elected head of government in Pakistan to give birth while in office in 1990.

HM The Queen, Britain's longest reigning monarch with over 66 years on the throne, Queen Elizabeth has four children, eight grandchildren and seven great-grandchildren.

Jacinda Ardern, in 2018 the 40th Prime Minister of New Zealand became the second elected ruler to give birth while in office.

Queen Victoria, ruled over the British Empire while producing nine children.

Mirror mirror on the wall,
I am my mother after all.

"All women become like their mothers. That is their tragedy. No man does. That is his."

OSCAR WILDE

"*The clocks were striking midnight and the rooms were very still as a figure glided quietly from bed to bed, smoothing a coverlid here, settling a pillow there, and pausing to look long and tenderly at each unconscious face, to kiss each with lips that mutely blessed, and to pray the fervent prayers which only mothers utter.*"

LOUISA MAY ALCOTT
From *Little Women*

Up until 1965 the average woman had more than five children. Today the global average has halved to 2.5 children per mother.

UNICEF states that, on average, about 353,000 babies are born in the world every day. That's 245 babies a minute!

"*I am sure that if the mothers of various nations could meet, there would be no more wars.*"

E.M. FORSTER
From *Howard's End*

According to Jungian archetypes, there are three essential aspects of the mother:

1. Her cherishing goodness

2. Her emotionality

3. Her depths

"Only mother can think of the future – because they gave birth to it in their children."

MAXIM GORKY

Multi-tasking + love = motherhood

Motherhood brings out your inner songbird. Meal times, bed times, bath times – all are now great opportunities to break into song and keep your little one happy!

"Mothers and children are human beings and they will sometimes do the wrong thing."

MAURICE SENDAK

Motherhood is...

- Mixing up the dish washer and washing machine.

- Not brushing your hair for a week.

- Treading on lego.

- Full of laughter.

- Full of tears.

- Rediscovering your favourite childhood games.

- Working out how to get stains out of everything.

- Pure joy.

- An adventure.

"Motherhood is the only place you can experience heaven and hell at the same time."

ANONYMOUS

Motherhood is the reason,
not the excuse.

Anyone who says motherhood is easy, clearly isn't doing it properly.

Motherhood is like running a marathon but without the ribbon and the free t-shirt.

"*Children are the anchors*
of a mother's life."

SOPHOCLES

Motherhood can be a dichotomy between joy and drudgery.

Mothers often embody two contrasting and opposing activities and emotions at the same moment.

Emotional – practical

Tired – resolute

Worried – hopeful

Impatient – patient

Chaotic – fun

Overwhelmed – persevering

Being a mother is knowing when to give them their freedom.

Motherhood is learning about strengths you didn't know you had and fears you didn't know existed.

Remember, they do grow up.

BIBLIOGRAPHY

Alcott, Louisa May., *Little Women* (1879)

Chapin, E.H., *Living Words* (HardPress, 2013)

Eliot, George., *Daniel Deronda* (1876)

Forster, E.M., *Howard's End* (1910)

Friday, Nancy., *My Mother, Myself* (HarperCollins, 2010)

Fromm, Eric., *The Art of Loving* (Thorsons, 1995)

Joyce, James., *A Portrait of the Artist as a Young Man* (1977)

Salinger, J.D., *The Catcher in the Rye* (1951)

Thackeray, William Makepeace., *Vanity Fair* (1848)

Tolstoy, Leo., *Childhood, Boyhood, Youth* (1854)

Twain, Mark., *Autobiography of Mark Twain, Volume 1* (1907)

FURTHER READING

Angelou, Maya., *I Know Why the Caged Bird Sings* (Virago, 1969)

Fry, Stephen., *Mythos* (Penguin, 2018)

Gold, Claudia., *Queen, Empress, Concubine* (Quercus, 2008)

Jung., *Four archetypes* (Routledge Classics, 2003)

Rowan, Tiddy., *The Little Book of Love* (Quadrille, 2015)

QUOTES ARE TAKEN FROM:

Abraham Lincoln was the 16th President of the United States.

Agatha Christie was an author of detective fiction whose books have sold over 2 billion copies.

Anne Lander was a 20th century American agony aunt.

Anna Jordan is a contemporary English playwright.

Annie Lennox is an internationally acclaimed Scottish singer and songwriter.

Barbara Kingsolver is an American novelist whose most famous work is *The Poisonwood Bible*.

Cardinal Gaspard Mermillod was a 19th century Swiss catholic cardinal.

C.S. Lewis was an English writer and author of *The Chronicles of Narnia*.

Debra Gilbert Rosenberg is a clinical psychotherapist.

Dorothy Canfield was a 20th century American education reformer and social activist.

Edgar Allen Poe was an 19th century Gothic novelist.

E.H. Chapin was an American preacher and poet.

Emily Dickinson was an American poet.

Eric Fromm was a 20th century German American psychologist.

Erna Bombeck was a 20th century American humourist.

George Eliot (the pen name of Mary Anne Evans) was a Victorian writer whose best-known work is *Middlemarch*.

Groucho Marx was an American comedian.

Helen Steiner Rice was a 20th century American poet.

Henry Ward Beecher was a social reformer.

Honoré de Balzac was a 19th century French novelist and playwright.

James Joyce was an Irish author, famous for penning *Ulysses*.

Isadora Duncan was a 20th century dancer.

J.D. Salinger was an American writer and author of *The Catcher in the Rye*.

Jerome K. Jerome was an English writer and humorist best known for *Three Men in a Boat*.

Jessica Lange is an American film actress.

Lance Conrad is a contemporary author.

Leo Tolstoy was a 19th century Russian writer and author of *War and Peace* and *Anna Karenina*.

Lin Yutang was 20th century Chinese writer and philosopher.

Marcel Proust was the 19th century French author of *Rembrance of Things Past*.

Margaret Culkin Banning was a 20th century American novelist and advocate of women's rights.

Maurice Sendak was an illustrator and writer of children's books.

Maxim Gorky was a Soviet social realist writer.

Nancy Friday was a 20th century American author.

Oprah Winfrey is an American chat show host.

Oscar Wilde was a 19th century poet and playwright.

Pablo Picasso was a 20th century Spanish painter.

Phyllis Diller was an American actress and stand up comedian.

Robert Browning was a Victorian English poet who mastered the form of the monologue.

Rudyard Kipling was an English writer whose work included *The Jungle Book*.

Samuel Taylor Coleridge was a poet and founder of The Romantic movement in 19th century England.

Sophocles was an Ancient Greek tragedian.

Stevie Wonder is an internationally renowned singer and songwriter.

Thich Nhat Hanh is a Vietnamese monk.

Thomas C. Haliburton was a 19th century Canadian author.

Victor Hugo was a French writer and author of *Les Misérables*.

Viv Apple is a 21st century poet.

Wangechi Mutu is a contemporary international artist.

Washington Irving was a 19th century American historian.

W.E.B. Du Bois was an American sociologist and historian.

W.H. Davies was a wandering Welsh tramp and poet.

William Makepeace Thackeray was a 19th century writer and author of *Vanity Fair*.

Publishing Director Sarah Lavelle
Editor Harriet Butt
Assistant Editor Harriet Webster
Words Alison Davies, Joanna Gray
Series Designer Emily Lapworth
Designer Monika Adamczyk
Production Director Vincent Smith
Production Controller Sinead Hering

Published in 2019 by Quadrille,
an imprint of Hardie Grant Publishing

Quadrille
52-54 Southwark Street
London SE1 1UN
quadrille.com

Cataloguing in Publication Data: a catalogue record for
this book is available from the British Library.

ISBN 978 1 78713 377 8

Printed in China